A Year of Sikh Festivals

Flora York

W

FRANKLIN WATTS
LONDON · SYDNEY

First published in 2008
by Franklin Watts

Copyright © 2008 Franklin Watts

Franklin Watts
338 Euston Road
London NW1 3BH

Franklin Watts Australia
Level 17/207 Kent Street
Sydney NSW 2000

Dewey classification: 294.6
ISBN: 978 0 7496 8345 0

Art Direction: Jonathan Hair   Designer (original edition): Joelle Wheelwright
Map (p.7): Aziz Khan   Picture Research: Diana Morris
Faith Consultant: Jagbir Jhutti-Johal

Produced for Franklin Watts by Storeybooks.
The text of this book is based on *Sikh Festivals Through the Year* by Anita Ganeri
Copyright © Franklin Watts 2003.

Acknowledgements
The publishers would like to thank the following for permission to reproduce photos
in this book: Gordon Clements/ Axiom: 25tr; B. Dhanjal/ Trip: 22tr; Dinodia Photo
Library: 26b; Paul Doyle/ Photofusion: 13t, 20t; Paul Gapper/ World Religions Photo
Library: 26t; Arvind Garg/ Corbis: 15tl; Prem Kapoor/ World Religions Photo Library:
19b; Christine Osborne/ World Religions Photo Library: front cover, 10bl, 17t, 23t,
24t; H. Rogers/ Trip: 6c, 10tr, 11c, 16t, 18r, 21t, 22bl, 25bl, 27t; Trip: 8b, 14t.

Printed in China

Franklin Watts is a division of Hachette Children's Books,
an Hachette Livre UK company.
www.hachettelivre.co.uk

Contents

Words printed in **bold** are explained in the glossary.

Sikhs

Sikhs are people who follow the Sikh religion. They believe in God. 'Sikh' means 'learner'. Sikhism began in India, and that is where most Sikhs live today. Sikhs meet to **worship** God in a building called a gurdwara. They take off their shoes and cover their heads.

▼ *The Golden Temple in Amritsar, India.*

How Sikhism began

In India 500 years ago, there were two main religions: **Hinduism** and **Islam**. They often didn't agree about what to believe and how to live.

A **holy** man called Nanak lived in Punjab, in north-west India. He had a **vision** of God, and started spreading the message that people had to respect other people's religious beliefs.

Nanak was the first Sikh Guru, or teacher.

Sikh beliefs

Sikhs try to remember God in everything they do, and live a good life. They believe that you should help other people without thinking about yourself. This is called *seva*, or service. They also believe that God sees everyone as equal, whether they are rich or poor.

In the gurdwara

When Sikhs meet for worship in the gurdwara, they sit on the floor. During the service, they listen to readings from the Sikh holy book, sing **shabads** (hymns), and say prayers. Afterwards, they share a vegetarian meal called **langar**. People take it in turns to cook and serve the meal.

▲ *Sikhs worshipping in a gurdwara.*

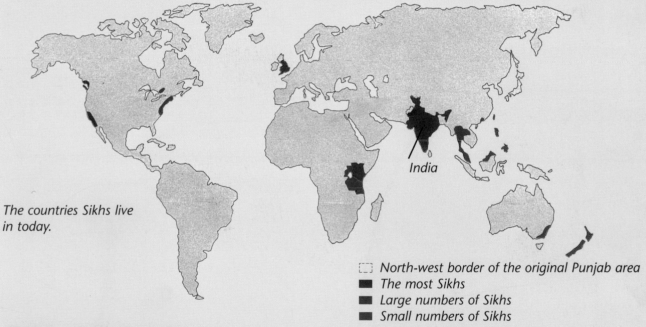

The countries Sikhs live in today.

India

:¨: *North-west border of the original Punjab area*
■ *The most Sikhs*
■ *Large numbers of Sikhs*
■ *Small numbers of Sikhs*

Sikh festivals

At a festival, people gather together to mark or **celebrate** a special occasion or an important event. The festival may have its own **customs** and **ceremonies**.

Sikhs hold festivals to remember times in the lives of the ten Gurus (see page 8). Other festivals look back at things that happened in Sikh history.

The Sikh Gurus

A Guru is a teacher **inspired** by God. Guru Nanak was the first Sikh Guru. Before he died, he chose one of his followers to become the next Guru and pass on his teachings. After Nanak's death, there were nine more Gurus.

▼ *The ten Sikh Gurus.*

The ten Sikh Gurus

The Gurus taught Sikhs how to live in a way that brought them closer to God.

1 **Guru Nanak** (1469–1539). Taught the basic Sikh beliefs and established many customs.

2 **Guru Angad Dev** (1504–1552).

3 **Guru Amar Das** (1479–1574). Spoke out against the unfair treatment of women.

4 **Guru Ram Das** (1534–1581). Founded the city of Amritsar, a famous centre of the Sikh **faith**.

5 **Guru Arjan Dev** (1563–1606). Built the Golden Temple (see page 6).

6 **Guru Hargobind** (1595–1644).

7 **Guru Har Rai** (1630–1661). Set up hospitals that gave out free medicines and treatment.

8 **Guru Har Krishan** (1656–1664). Cared for the sick until he died of smallpox at the age of eight.

9 **Guru Tegh Bahadur** (1621–1675). Gave his life to allow people to follow their faith without fear.

10 **Guru Gobind Singh** (1666–1708). Set up the *Khalsa* (see pages 20–23).

▲ *A* granthi *reading from the Guru Granth Sahib.*

Gurpurbs and jore melas

Sikhs have two kinds of festivals. *Gurpurbs* remember events in the lives of the ten Gurus. *Jore melas* celebrate other times in Sikh history and are less serious occasions.

The Guru Granth Sahib

The Sikhs' holy book is called the Guru Granth Sahib. It is made up of hymns. Most were written by the Gurus.

Sikhs believe that the Guru Granth Sahib is the word of God, and they treat it with great respect. In the gurdwara, it is kept on a platform under a canopy, and covered with a cloth.

The person who looks after the Guru Granth Sahib is called the *granthi*. He or she also reads it out at services.

Guru Nanak

In November, Sikhs remember Guru Nanak's birthday with a *gurpurb* (see pages 12–13). This is one of the most important times of the year for Sikhs.

Guru Nanak, who started ▶ the Sikh religion.

▼ A gurdwara near Lahore in Pakistan.

Nanak's birth

Nanak was born in 1469 in the village of Talwandi, near Lahore (now in Pakistan). His family were Hindus.

As a boy, Nanak was very religious. According to Sikh stories, some things that happened in his childhood showed that he was a special person.

Nanak becomes a Guru

When Nanak was about 30 years old, God told him to teach people how to live good lives.

From that time, Nanak became known as 'Guru Nanak'. The things he taught people became a new religion, called Sikhism.

Following God

Nanak told his friends that all religions are different ways of worshipping the same God, so people should respect other religions.

Nanak said that his teachings would help people to draw closer to God. He taught that everyone was equal, and it was important to share with others.

▲ *Guru Nanak (with halo) and his friend, Mardana (seated).*

Nanak's travels

Guru Nanak travelled around the country, teaching about God and the way God wanted people to live. His Muslim friend, Mardana, travelled with him. He was a musician. Guru Nanak often used poetry to explain his teachings. Mardana set the poems to music. Guru Nanak chose Guru Angad Dev to be the next Guru.

Gurpurbs

A *gurpurb* that marks a Guru's birthday is celebrated in a certain way in the gurdwara. There are also street processions.

▲ *Reading the Guru Granth Sahib.*

Akhand Path

At the gurdwara, there is a special, non-stop reading of the whole of the Guru Granth Sahib. Readers take it in turns to read aloud, and it takes about 48 hours. This is called an *Akhand Path*.

Many Sikhs pop in to listen to the reading for a while, then go home.

Gurdwara service

The *Akhand Path* finishes early on the day of the *gurpurb*. Then there is a service. People sing hymns that praise the Guru, and listen to talks about the meaning of the *gurpurb*. Afterwards, everyone shares *langar* (a vegetarian meal).

◀ Langar *after the service.*

▲ *Men dressed as the* Panj Piare.

Processions

There may be processions through the streets to celebrate a *gurpurb*. Five **baptised** Sikh men dressed in orange or yellow lead the procession. A decorated float follows them, carrying the Guru Granth Sahib.

Members of the gurdwara walk behind the float, singing hymns. Some may hand out sweets or drinks to the watching crowd.

Five brave men

Guru Gobind Singh found five brave Sikhs who were willing to die for their faith (see pages 20–21). They became known as the *Panj Piare*, or five beloved ones. They were the first members of a **community** set up by Guru Gobind Singh called the *Khalsa*.

The five men who lead the procession through the streets on a *gurpurb* are dressed as the *Panj Piare*.

They wear an orange or yellow robe, a blue sash and a turban. A turban is a long piece of cloth that is wrapped around the head. They carry a special sword called the kirpan, which **symbolises** courage.

Guru Tegh Bahadur

Sikhs remember the death of Guru Tegh Bahadur with a *gurpurb* in November. The Guru gave up his life for his beliefs, when he was killed for refusing to change his religion. Sikhs believe that his strong faith is an example to all.

Guru Tegh Bahadur. ▶

The Guru is executed

The emperor who ruled India wanted everyone to become a Muslim. Many people who refused were killed.

A group of Hindu holy men asked Guru Tegh Bahadur for help. The Guru told them to tell the emperor that if he could persuade Guru Tegh Bahadur to become a Muslim, all Hindus would change faith too.

The emperor offered the Guru all sorts of riches to become a Muslim. But Guru Tegh Bahadur refused. The emperor ordered the Guru's execution.

Remembering

Guru Tegh Bahadur's death is remembered by an *Akhand Path* in the gurdwara, a service and street processions.

The Guru was killed in Delhi, the capital of India. The Sis Ganj Sahib Gurdwara has been built where he died.

◀ *The Sis Ganj Sahib Gurdwara in Delhi, India.*

Make a romalla

When the Guru Granth Sahib is not in use, it is covered with a decorated cloth called a *romalla*. On special occasions, Sikhs make an **offering** of a *romalla*. To make a *romalla*:

1. Cut a piece of coloured cloth measuring about 1 x 1.25 m. Turn over the edges, and sew or stick them down.

2. Sew or stick gold braid around the edges of the cloth.

3. Decorate the cloth with fabric pens or paints. Draw geometric patterns, flowers and leaves.

Draw a Sikh symbol, the '*Ik Onkar*' (right). It means 'There is only one God'.

Guru Gobind Singh

In January, Sikhs in India celebrate the birthday of Guru Gobind Singh with a *gurpurb*. Sikhs in other countries celebrate on the nearest Sunday.

Guru Gobind Singh. ▶

All about Guru Gobind Singh

Gobind Singh was born in 1666 in Patna, India.

His father was Guru Tegh Bahadur (see pages 14–15).

When he was nine, his father died. He became the tenth and last Guru.

Guru Gobind Singh was kind, clever and brave. He fought many battles to protect the Sikhs.

Just before he died in 1708, he told the Sikhs that from then on, the Guru Granth Sahib would guide them instead of a human Guru.

The Khalsa

Guru Gobind Singh created the *Khalsa* (see pages 20–21). Sikhs who became members of the *Khalsa* were baptised as a sign that they had joined. They drank a mixture of sugar and water called *amrit*. The Guru drank it too. To be a true Sikh today, Sikhs should also join the *Khalsa* and be baptised (see page 22).

Celebrations

To celebrate the *gurpurb*, there is a procession. Five men dress as the *Panj Piare* and the Guru Granth Sahib is carried on a float. Gurdwaras are decorated with banners and flowers. There is a service in the gurdwara to remember Guru Gobind Singh.

A procession in London. ▶

Karah parshad

Karah parshad is a sweet mixture given out to people at the end of a Sikh service. To make it, you will need:

1 cup of sugar
1 cup of unsalted butter
1 cup of semolina
½ cup of water

1. Melt the butter in a pan over a low heat. Add the semolina. Cook for a few minutes until golden.

2. Mix in the sugar and the water, and stir until thick. Leave to cool.

Hola Mohalla

The festival of *Hola Mohalla* is in February or March. It is a *jore mela* (see page 9). It is mainly celebrated in Anandapur in India, where it began in 1680.

A Sikh dressed as a Nihang, *or Sikh warrior.* ▶

The first Hola Mohalla

Hindus have a spring festival called *Holi*. Guru Gobind Singh decided that Sikhs should have their own festival on the day after *Holi*. It was called *Hola Mohalla*.

He called Sikhs together to practise their fighting skills. They needed to be able to defend their faith against the **Mughal** rulers of India. So the Sikhs practised with their weapons, and pretended to fight battles.

Celebrating today

In Anandapur today, there are displays of martial arts, sports matches and music and poetry competitions. People sing hymns and listen to religious talks.

There is also a big procession. Sikhs dressed as the *Panj Piare* carry the flags of the local gurdwaras.

Some Sikhs in other countries also celebrate *Hola Mohalla*.

▼ *Showing martial arts at Hola Mohalla.*

Kabaddi

Kabaddi is an Indian game that Sikhs like to play. There are often *kabaddi* competitions around *Hola Mohalla* time.

There are two teams of players. Each team tries to get a player to break through a row of members of the other team.

The other team tries to stop him by wrestling him to the ground.

As the player breaks through the line, he has to say '*Kabaddi*' for as long as he can before taking another breath.

Baisakhi

The festival of *Baisakhi* remembers the time when Guru Gobind Singh set up the *Khalsa*.

Baisakhi is in April. It is a *jore mela* (see page 9). Sikhs gather to celebrate their faith. In India, it is also the start of the Sikh New Year.

▲ *Happy Baisakhi!*

The first Baisakhi

In 1699, Guru Gobind Singh called all the Sikhs to Anandapur. The Guru asked if any of them were ready to die for their faith. Finally, a man stepped forward. The Guru took him into his tent.

Then the Guru came out, with blood dripping from his sword. The crowd was horrified. This happened four more times, as four more brave men answered the Guru's challenge.

What happened next

The crowd was amazed when Guru Gobind Singh led the men out of his tent alive. He declared that their bravery proved how strongly they believed in Sikhism. He said they would now be called the *Panj Piare* (five beloved ones).

The *Panj Piare* were the first members of the *Khalsa*. They were religious men, but also a fighting force ready to defend Sikhs and people of other faiths.

The Guru and the Panj Piare. ▶

Five Ks

Guru Gobind Singh asked Sikhs who joined the *Khalsa* to wear five items. Sikhs still do this today. The items are known as the Five Ks because they all begin with a 'K'.

1. *Kesh* – uncut hair. Men keep their hair wrapped in a turban.

2. *Kangha* – a small wooden comb that keeps long hair tidy.

3. *Kara* – a steel bracelet worn on the right wrist.

4. *Kirpan* – a small sword.

5. *Kachera* – a special pair of shorts, worn as underwear.

These items are symbols of obedience to God, honesty, faith in God, and being ready to fight for your Sikh beliefs.

Celebrating Baisakhi

Gurdwaras hold a *Baisakhi* service, with prayers, hymns and talks. There is an *Akhand Path* (see page 12). In some places there are street processions.

A procession at Baisakhi. ▶

Joining the Khalsa

Many young Sikhs join the *Khalsa* at *Baisakhi*. First, they bathe and put on the Five Ks.

They are baptised in a ceremony at the gurdwara, where they drink *amrit* five times. It is also sprinkled on their eyes and hair. They promise to follow the teachings of the Gurus.

◀ *Preparing* amrit, *a special mixture of sugar and water.*

Member of the Khalsa

When Sikhs join the *Khalsa* today, they promise to live by certain rules for the rest of their lives. There are religious acts that they must perform each day. They must wear the Five Ks at all times.

Men take 'Singh' as part of their name, which means 'lion' and is a sign of courage. Women take the name 'Kaur', which means 'princess' and shows that they are important.

Changing the gurdwara flag at Baisakhi. ▶

Khanda

Every gurdwara flies the Sikh flag, which is called the *Nishan Sahib* flag.

It has a symbol called the *khanda* on it. This shows a double-edged sword in a circle, and two crossed swords. These all symbolise different parts of God's power.

Make a Nishan Sahib flag

1. Cut out a triangle of yellow cloth.

2. Cut out a *khanda* symbol from black cloth and stick or sew it on the triangle. It is easier to make each part of the *khanda* symbol separately.

3. Get a piece of dowelling (a rounded stick) for the flagpole. Glue the edge of the flag around it.

4. Make another *khanda* symbol from card covered in cooking foil. Glue this to the top of the flagpole.

Guru Arjan Dev

In June, there is a *gurpurb* to mark the death of Guru Arjan Dev. In 1606 he was killed by the Mughal emperor of India because he stood by his Sikh beliefs.

Guru Arjan Dev died for his ▶ *religious beliefs.*

ਸ੍ਰੀ ਗੁਰੂ ਅਰਜਨਦੇਵ ਜੀ

The story of Guru Arjan Dev

The emperor was a Muslim and did not like the Sikh religion. He suspected that Guru Arjan Dev was plotting against him and ordered him to pay him a huge sum of money. He also told the Guru to change the words of the Guru Granth Sahib.

Guru Arjan Dev refused to do either of these things. He said that he only had money for the poor. He also said that the Guru Granth Sahib was holy and no one was allowed to alter it. He was arrested and put in prison.

The Guru dies

The emperor had the Guru tortured. Also, he wouldn't give the Guru any food and water.

But despite this, the Guru would not agree to the emperor's demands. Finally, the emperor's men pushed him into the river and he drowned.

The river where the Guru drowned. ▶

◀ *Sikhs serving drinks to remember the Guru's death.*

Cool drinks

For the *gurpurb*, Sikhs listen to stories about Guru Arjan Dev. They also serve drinks to passers-by. It is a reminder of when the Guru was tortured by not being allowed water to drink.

The drinks are also a way of looking after other people and so serving God.

Divali

Divali is the festival of lights. This *jore mela* (see page 9) is in October or November. It remembers Guru Hargobind's return to his home in Amritsar.

Sikhs in London lighting ▶ *candles for* Divali.

The story of Divali

Guru Hargobind was the son of Guru Arjan Dev, who was killed by the Muslim emperor. He began to train an army.

One day, Guru Hargobind saved the emperor from a tiger. The two men became friends. Then the emperor fell ill. He needed a holy man to help him get better, so he asked the Guru to go to Gwalior Fort to pray for him.

In the fort, Guru Hargobind found 52 Hindu princes who were prisoners.

Hindu Divali

Hindus celebrate *Divali* for a different reason.

They remember the story of a god and goddess, Rama and Sita. They were living in **exile** but then won a battle and returned home to become king and queen. At *Divali*, Hindus light lamps to guide Rama and Sita.

The Guru's cloak

The emperor got better and told the Guru that he could leave the fort. But the Guru said he would not go unless the Hindu princes could leave too. The emperor said that he could take only the princes who could hold on to his cloak when he went through the gate. The clever Guru had a cloak made with 52 long tassels. All the princes were able to leave!

Guru Hargobind leading the ▶ *princes out of Gwalior Fort.*

▼ Divali *at the Golden Temple.*

Celebrating Divali

The Sikhs in Amritsar decorated the Golden Temple with lights to welcome the Guru back. They still do this every year to remember the Guru's happy return.

Sikhs everywhere put lights in their homes and gurdwaras. They go to services in the gurdwara.

Festival calendar

Month	Festival
October/November	Guru Nanak's birthday
November/December	Guru Tegh Bahadur's death
December/January	Guru Gobind Singh's birthday
February/March	*Hola Mohalla*
13/14 April	*Baisakhi*
June	Guru Arjan Dev's death
October/November	*Divali*

Calendars used by Sikhs

In the Hindu **lunar calendar**, the months are:

Magha	(January/February)
Phalguna	(February/March)
Chaitra	(March/April)
Vaisakha	(April/May)
Jyeshtha	(May/June)
Ashadha	(June/July)
Shravana	(July/August)
Badra	(August/September)
Ashvina	(September/October)
Karttika	(October/November)
Margashirsha	(November/December)
Pausha	(December/January)

In the *Nanakshahi* calendar, the months are:

Katik	(October/November)
Maghar	(November/December)
Poh	(December/January)
Magh	(January/February)
Phagan	(February/March)
Chet	(March/April)
Vaisakh	(April/May)
Jeth	(May/June)
Harh	(June/July)
Sawan	(July/August)
Bhadon	(August/September)
Asu	(September/October)

In the *Nanakshahi* calendar, the year begins in *Katik* with Guru Nanak's birthday.

Glossary

Baptised; baptism Sikhs are baptised at a baptism ceremony to become members of the *Khalsa*. They drink *amrit*, and it is also sprinkled on them.

Celebrate To be pleased and happy about something, and to have special festivities, or celebrations, to mark the occasion.

Ceremonies Occasions where you do special things to mark an event.

Community A group of people. It can also mean the people living in a particular area.

Customs Habits or traditions.

Exile Being forced to live away from your home or country.

Faith Belief; a religion. To have faith in God means to believe that God will always look after you.

Hinduism An ancient religion that began in India at least 4,000 years ago. Followers are called Hindus. Most Indians are Hindus.

Holy A person who is holy is extremely good and devoted to religion and God. Items that are holy or sacred are things connected to a religion or god which are very special and important.

Inspired Influenced in a way that makes you full of enthusiasm.

Islam The religion of the Muslims. Muslims are the second biggest religious group in India. The Mughal rulers of India were Muslims.

Khalsa A group of Sikhs founded by Guru Gobind Singh in 1699. The word 'Khalsa' means 'pure'. A Sikh who decides to join the *Khalsa* is baptised and has to live by certain rules.

Langar A vegetarian meal that everyone shares at the end of a service in the gurdwara. It is prepared and served in a room of the same name.

Lunar calendar A calendar based on the moon. It only has 354 days.

Mughal (Also Mogul.) A member of a family of Muslim rulers of India, who ruled from 1526–1857.

Offering Things that are given as a mark of respect.

Shabads Hymns found in the Guru Granth Sahib. Hymns are songs that praise God.

Symbolises Stands for something else.

Vision A picture in your mind.

Worship To show great love and respect for someone. In a religion, this can include singing hymns, saying prayers, reading sacred writings and making offerings.

Further resources

Websites

www.ngfl.ac.uk/re/welcometo
thegurdwara.htm
Tour of a gurdwara.

atschool.eduweb.co.uk/carolrb/
sikhism/sikhism1.html
All about Sikhism.

www.sikhnet.com/s/SikhStories
Sikh stories.

www.thegrid.org.uk/learning/re
/virtual/sikh/index.shtml
Tour of a gurdwara.

www.sikhs.org/golden/index.
html
Pictures of the Golden Temple in
Amritsar.

Note to parents and teachers: Every effort has been made by the Publishers to ensure that these websites are suitable for children, that they are of the highest educational value, and that they contain no inappropriate or offensive material. However, because of the nature of the Internet, it is impossible to guarantee that the contents of these sites will not be altered. We strongly advise that Internet access is supervised by a responsible adult.

Index